18 Reproducible Music Worksheets
D. Brian Weese

Credits
Editor: Nicole LeGrand
Cover Design and Illustrations: Jeff Richards

Permission-to-Reproduce Notice

Heritage Music Press
A division of The Lorenz Corporation
PO Box 802
Dayton OH 45401
www.lorenz.com

Printed in the United States of America.

ISBN: 978-1-4291-3700-3

HERITAGE
MUSIC PRESS
A Lorenz Company • www.lorenz.com

Contents

Name: _____   Classroom Teacher: _____   Date: _____

3 Beat Maze

Directions: Beginning at the top left corner of the maze and moving left to right in each row, circle or color in the groups of squares that equal three beats when added together. Use the table below for help as needed. The number to the left of each row indicates the number of three-beat groups you will find in that row.

When completed correctly, the squares not marked will form a path from the time signature at the top to the treble clef sign at the bottom of the maze.

The first row has been done for you.

Name: _____ Classroom Teacher: _____ Date: _____

4 Beat Maze

Directions: Beginning at the top left corner of the maze and moving left to right in each row, circle or color in the groups of squares that equal four beats when added together. Use the table below for help as needed. The number to the left of each row indicates the number of four-beat groups you will find in that row.

When completed correctly, the squares not marked will form a path from the time signature at the top to the treble clef sign at the bottom of the maze.

The first row has been done for you.

4

Name: _____   Classroom Teacher: _____   Date: _____

Composer Timeline Maze 1

Directions: Look at the timeline below. Using the information in the timeline, find a path from START to FINISH which proceeds chronologically and uses each name only once.

RENAIS-SANCE 1400–1600	BAROQUE 1600–1750		CLASSICAL 1730–1820						ROMANTIC 1830–1900		
Giovanni **Palestrina**	Antonio **Vivaldi**	Johann Sebastian **Bach**	Johann **Haydn**	Wolfgang Amadeus **Mozart**	Ludwig van **Beethoven**	Frederic **Chopin**	Giuseppe **Verdi**		Camille **Saint–Saëns**	Modest **Mussorgsky**	Pyotr **Tchaikovsky**
1525–1594	1678–1741	1685–1750	1737–1806	1756–1791	1770–1827	1810–1849	1813–1901		1835–1921	1839–1881	1840–1893

▼ **START**

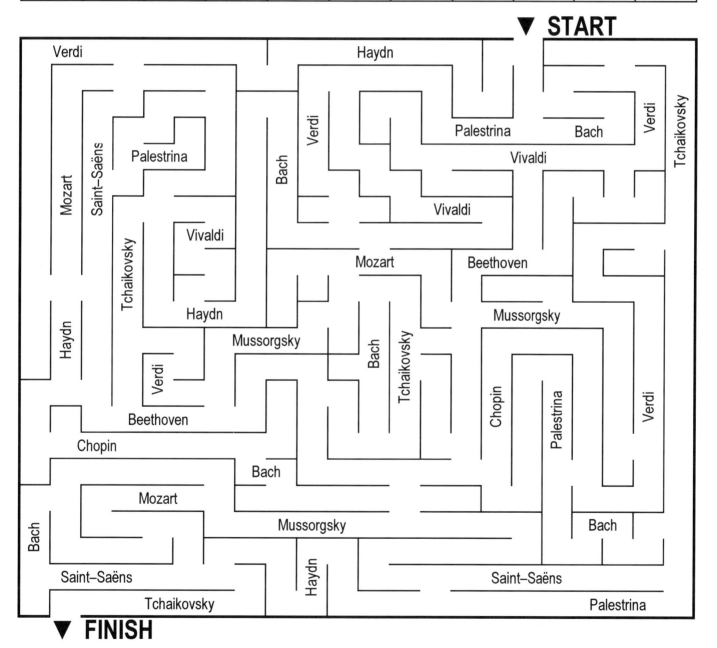

▼ **FINISH**

Composer Timeline Maze 2

Directions: Look at the timeline below. Using the information in the timeline, find a path from START to FINISH which proceeds chronologically and uses each name only once.

ROMANTIC 1830–1900						MODERN 1900–Current				
Edvard **Grieg**	John Philip **Sousa**	Claude **Debussy**	Gustav **Holst**	Zóltan **Kodály**	Sergei **Prokofiev**	George **Gershwin**	Aaron **Copland**	Carl **Orff**	Benjamin **Britten**	John **Williams**
1843–1907	1854–1932	1862–1918	1874–1934	1882–1967	1891–1953	1898–1937	1900–1990	1895–1982	1913–1976	b. 1932

▼ **START**

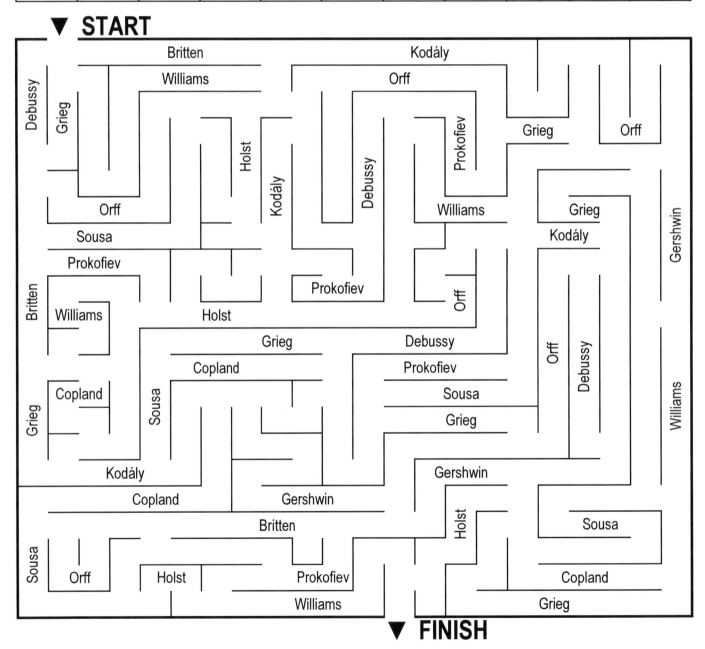

▼ **FINISH**

Create-a-Maze: Notespeller Maze

Directions: Using a ruler (if you have one), draw a line from each three-letter word to the staff that contains corresponding pitches. (Hint: write the names of the pitches under each staff before making matches.) Some words or staves may have more than one match and have been labeled with the number 2. You may only connect words with pitch sets (and some of the lines may cross), but no line should be drawn that connects a staff to a staff or word to word. When all matches have been made, a maze will be revealed. Complete the maze by drawing a path that begins with the arrow at the top of the maze, and follows a path of eighth notes to the bottom arrow.

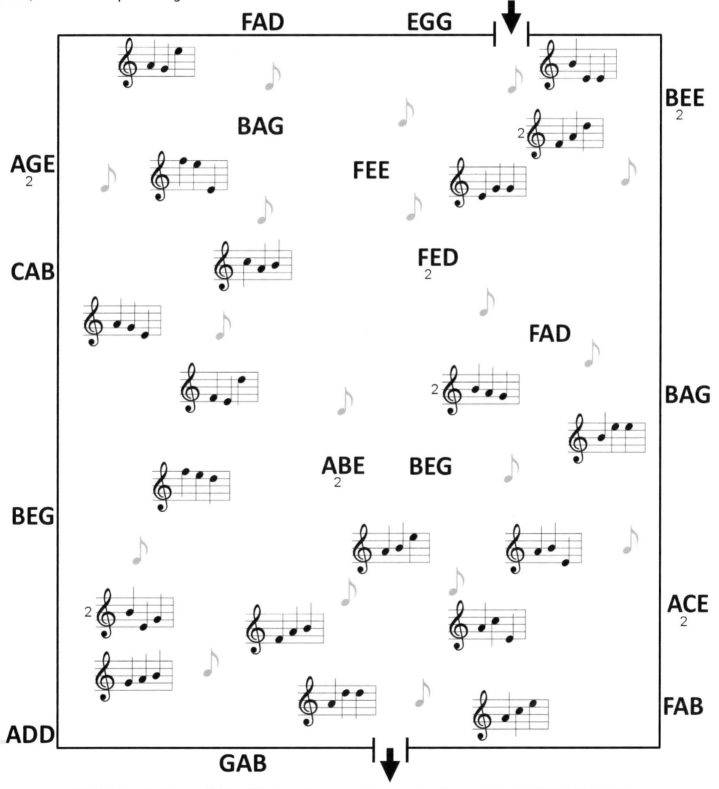

Name: _____ Classroom Teacher: _____ Date: _____

Instrument Family Maze

Directions: Beginning in the square below each instrument family's name, find a continuous path to the bottom of the maze using only instruments belonging to that family. You may move up, down, left, right, and diagonally. Each path will cross the path of another family at least once. Use the following key to color the paths:

Brass = yellow	Woodwind = blue	Strings = red	Percussion = green

Brass ▼   **Percussion** ▼   **Woodwinds** ▼   **Strings** ▼

Trumpet	Cymbals	Tuba	Trumpet	Bass Drum	Oboe	Trumpet	Clarinet	Cymbals	French Horn	Violin
French Horn	Bass Drum	Cello	Clarinet	Snare Drum	Trombone	Violin	Bassoon	Trumpet	Bass Drum	Cello
Bassoon	Trombone	Bassoon	String Bass	Triangle	Trumpet	Tuba	Flute	String Bass	Viola	French Horn
Triangle	Tuba	Violin	Flute	French Horn	Cymbals	Trombone	Violin	Clarinet	Oboe	Trumpet
Bass Drum	French Horn	Triangle	Viola	Clarinet	Snare Drum	Flute	Cello	Bass Drum	Snare Drum	Bassoon
Snare Drum	Clarinet	Trombone	Triangle	Cello	Triangle	Trumpet	French Horn	Viola	Cymbals	Clarinet
Bassoon	Violin	Trumpet	Bassoon	Flute	Trombone	Cymbals	Violin	Tuba	Flute	Triangle
French Horn	Clarinet	Bass Drum	Tuba	French Horn	Clarinet	Bass Drum	Cello	Clarinet	Trumpet	Cello
Trumpet	Viola	Cello	Violin	Oboe	Bassoon	Snare Drum	String Bass	French Horn	Bassoon	Bass Drum
Violin	Snare Drum	Cymbals	Bassoon	Viola	Cymbals	Violin	Flute	Trombone	Oboe	Violin
String Bass	Trombone	Clarinet	Tuba	Snare Drum	Cello	Oboe	Bassoon	Trumpet	Flute	Snare Drum
Violin	French Horn	Trumpet	Flute	Triangle	Trumpet	Clarinet	French Horn	Bass Drum	Clarinet	Cymbals

Strings ▼   **Percussion** ▼   **Brass** ▼   **Woodwinds** ▼

Matching Maze 1: Orchestral Instruments

Directions: Beginning with instrument #1, use a pencil to find the path connecting each instrument picture to its name. Once you have found the eight correct paths, use a different color to fill in each path. Paths may not intersect each other and will not travel down the same corridor. However, paths may cross over or under each other. For help see the examples to the right.

YES   NO   NO

Matching Maze 2: Music Terms and Symbols

Directions: Beginning with term #1 ("treble clef"), use a pencil to find the path connecting each music term to the corresponding music symbol. Once you have found the nine correct paths use a different color to fill in each path. Paths may not intersect each other and will not travel down the same corridor. However, paths may cross over or under each other. For help see the examples to the right.

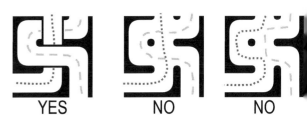

YES   NO   NO

Name: _____ Classroom Teacher: _____ Date: _____

Mixed Meter Maze 1

Directions: Time signatures tell us how many beats complete a measure and what kind of note equals one beat in that time signature. To find your way through this maze, look at the time signature and move the corresponding number of beats to complete one measure. You should then reach another time signature. (Remember, the top number tells how many beats are in a measure!) You may move up, down, left, and right, but no moving diagonally or overlapping your path! If you don't reach a time signature or you don't have enough beats before you get to another time signature, then you have reached a dead end. Trace the path back to the previous time signature and try again! The first path has been done for you.

♫ = 1 beat   ♩ = 1 beat   𝄽 = 1 beat

START

FINISH

Mixed Meter Maze 2

Directions: Time signatures tell us how many beats complete a measure and what kind of note equals one beat in that time signature. To find your way through this maze, look at the time signature and move the corresponding number of beats to complete one measure. You should then reach another time signature. (Remember, the top number tells how many beats are in a measure!) You may move up, down, left, and right, but no moving diagonally or overlapping your path! If you don't reach a time signature or you don't have enough beats before you get to another time signature, then you have reached a dead end. Trace the path back to the previous time signature and try again! The first path has been done for you.

Multiple Choice Maze: Dynamics

Directions: Inside each box in the maze below is an English or Italian music term. Surrounding the term are doorways leading to another box. Each doorway has a music symbol in it. You must travel through the doorway that has the corresponding symbol into the next box. Begin at the word START at the top left corner and continue until you reach FINISH in the bottom right corner.

START								
piano	*p*	forte	*pp*	mezzo piano	*mp*	soft	*p*	medium loud
pp		*f*		*f*		*pp*		*mf*
mezzo piano	*f*	medium loud	*mf*	loud	*ff*	very soft	*mp*	very soft
mf		*mp*		*mf*		*p*		*pp*
loud	*p*	piano	*f*	fortissimo	*ff*	mezzo forte	*p*	piano
f		*mp*		*mf*		*mf*		*mp*
very soft	*ff*	medium soft	*pp*	pianissimo	*ff*	fortissimo	*pp*	pianissimo
pp		*p*		*p*		*f*		*mf*
mezzo piano	*p*	pianissimo	*pp*	mezzo piano	*ff*	very loud	*mp*	loud
mp		*mf*		*mp*		*mp*		*f*
very loud	*ff*	mezzo forte	*ff*	forte	*pp*	soft	*p*	fortissimo
f		*f*		*f*		*mf*		*ff*
soft	*mp*	forte	*mp*	very loud	*ff*	mezzo forte	*mp*	FINISH

13

Pitch Maze 1: Note "Line" Up

Directions: Line notes are notes that have a line of the staff going through the middle of them. Help the soldier march his way back into "line" by following only squares containing line notes. You can move up, down, left, and right, but not diagonally. If you find yourself surrounded by space notes (notes that sit in the space between lines), then you have reached a dead end and must trace the path back and try a different route.

Bonus: Write the name of each line note you march through under the note.

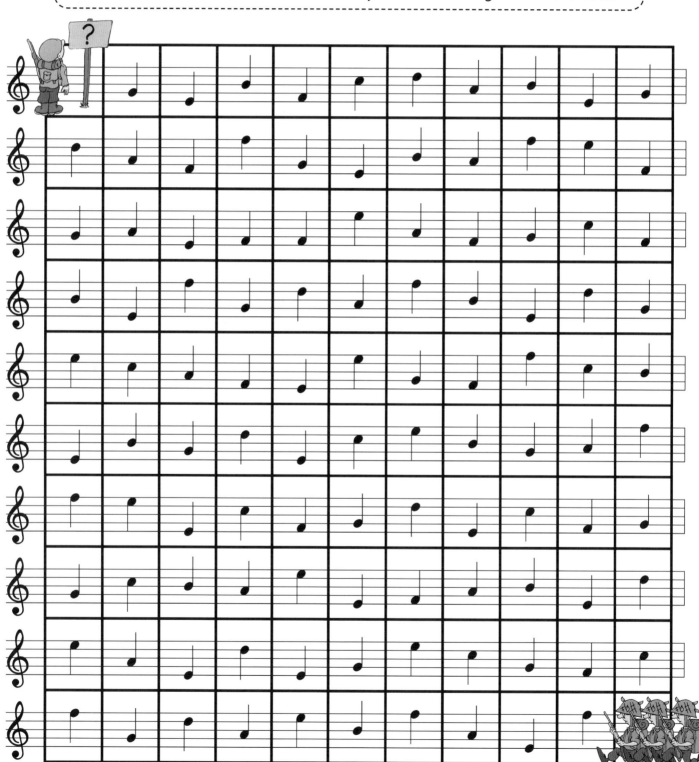

Pitch Maze 2: Flying Through "Spaces"

Directions: Space notes are notes that sit between two lines of the staff. Help the UFO navigate back to the wormhole by following squares containing only space notes. You can move up, down, left, and right, but not diagonally. If you find yourself surrounded by line notes (notes that have a line going through the middle of them), then you have reached a dead end and must trace the path back and try a different route.

Bonus: Write the name of each space note you fly through under the note.

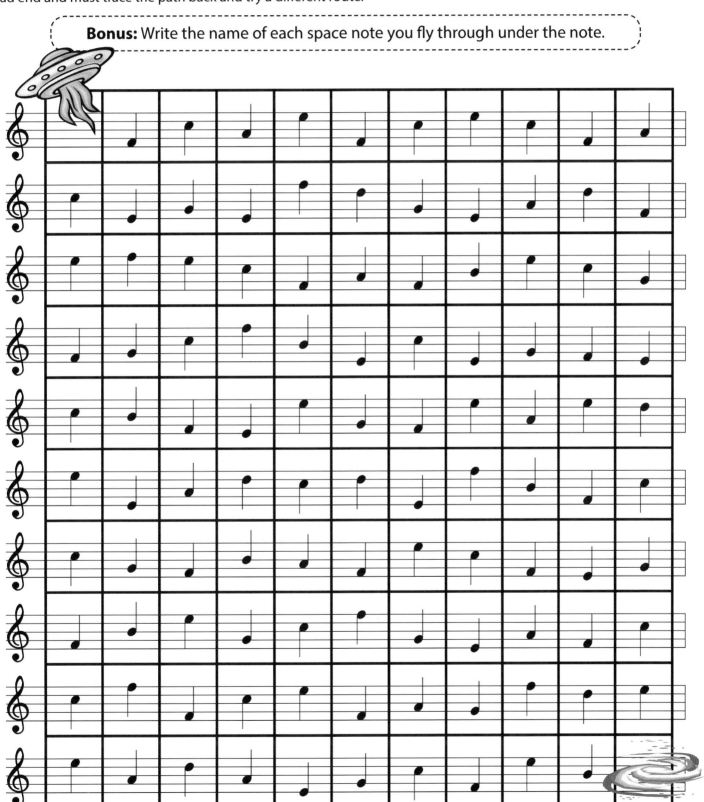

Rhythm Value Maze 1

Directions: In the maze below, find and color each square that contains a rhythm worth only one beat. When you are finished, you should see a complete path from top to bottom.

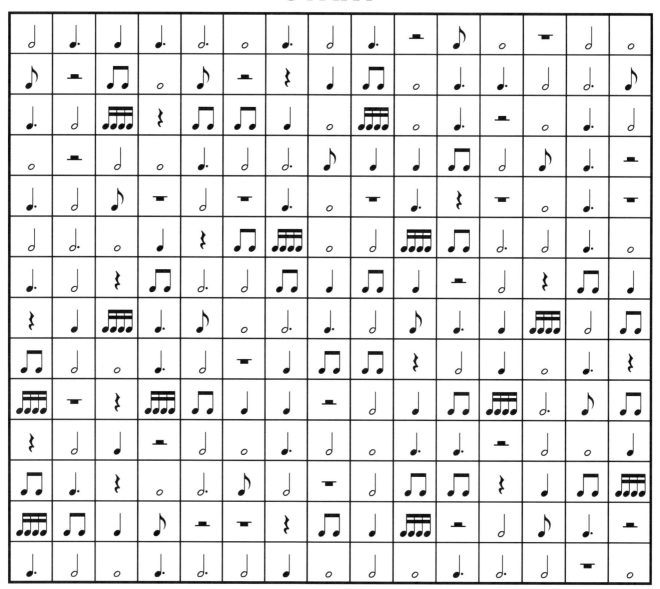

START

FINISH

Name: _____   Classroom Teacher: _____   Date: _____

Rhythm Value Maze 2

Directions: In the maze below, find and color each square that contains a rhythm consisting of two beats. When you are finished, you should see a complete path from top to bottom.

START

FINISH

Name: _____   Classroom Teacher: _____   Date: _____

Rhythm Value Maze 3

Directions: In the maze below, find and color each square that contains a rhythm consisting of three beats. When you are finished you, should see a complete path from top to bottom.

♪ = 1/2   ♩ = 1   ♫ = 1   𝅘𝅥𝅯𝅘𝅥𝅯𝅘𝅥𝅯𝅘𝅥𝅯 = 1   ♩. = 1 1/2   ♩ = 2   ♩. = 3   𝅝 = 4

𝄽 = 1   𝄼 = 2   𝄻 = 4

START

FINISH

Name: _____   Classroom Teacher: _____   Date: _____

Rhythm Value Maze 4

Directions: In the maze below, find and color each square that contains a rhythm consisting of four beats. When you are finished, you should see a complete path from top to bottom.

START

FINISH

19

Name: _____   Classroom Teacher: _____   Date: _____

Tempo Maze

Directions: The maze below is filled with Italian words relating to the tempo or speed of music. *Grave* is the term for a very, very slow speed (only 30 beats per minute). *Prestissimo* is the term for a very, very fast speed (200 beats per minute)! Using the chart below as a guide, find a path through the maze from start to finish that crosses each tempo marking only once in the order from slowest (*grave*) to fastest (*prestissimo*). If you encounter a tempo marking out of order then you've made a wrong turn and must go back and try again!

These Italian terms represent some of the more commonly used music tempo markings. The number below each term represents the number of beats per minute for that speed.

grave	*largo*	*adagio*	*andante*	*moderato*	*allegretto*	*allegro*	*vivace*	*presto*	*prestissimo*
≈30	≈45	≈55	≈75	≈90	≈100	≈120	≈135	≈175	≈200

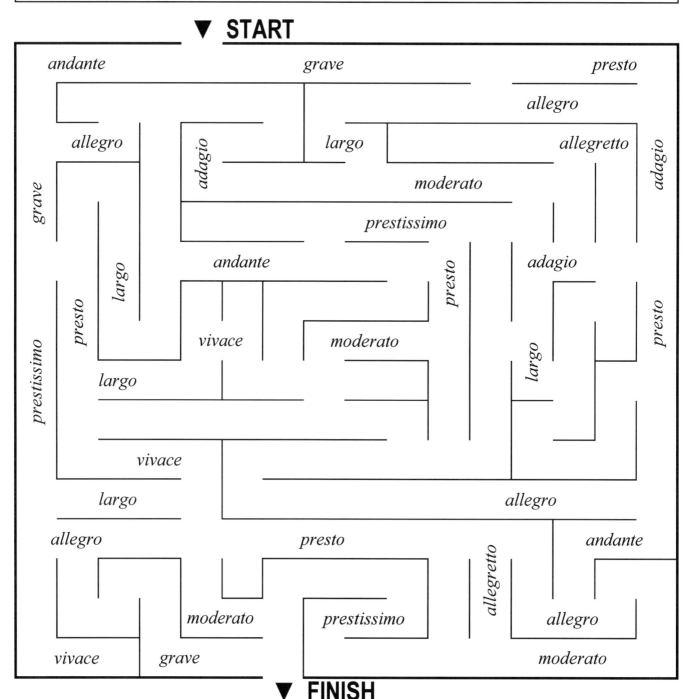

▼ START

▼ FINISH

Answer Key

3 Beat Maze
Page 3

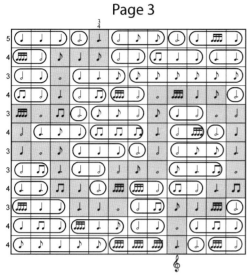

4 Beat Maze
Page 4

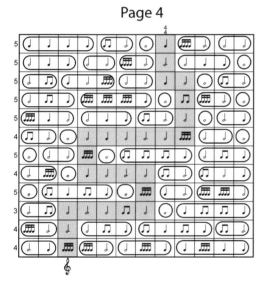

Composer Timeline Maze 1
Page 5

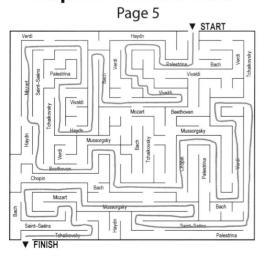

Composer Timeline Maze 2
Page 6

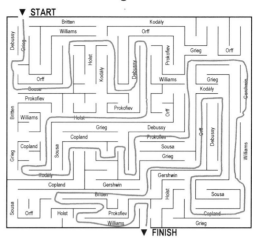

Create-a-Maze: Notespeller Maze
Page 7

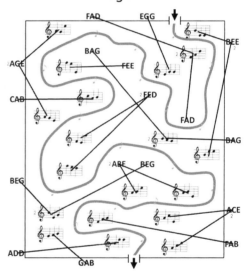

Instrument Family Maze
Page 8

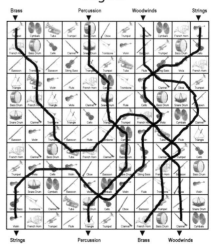

Answer Key

Matching Maze 1: Orchestral Instruments
Page 9

Matching Maze 2: Music Symbols and Terms - Page 10

Mixed Meter Maze 2
Page 12

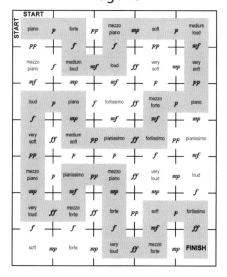

Multiple Choice Maze: Dynamics
Page 13

Mixed Meter Maze 1
Page 11

Pitch Maze 1: Note "Line" Up
Page 14

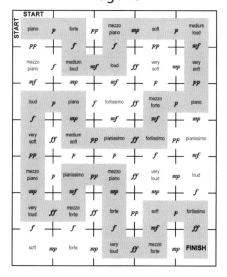

Answer Key

Pitch Maze 2: Flying Through "Spaces"
Page 15

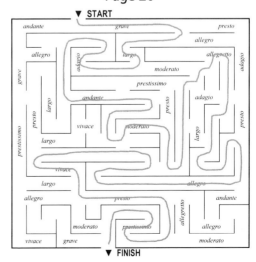

Rhythm Value Maze 3
Page 18

START

FINISH

Rhythm Value Maze 1
Page 16

START

FINISH

Rhythm Value Maze 4
Page 19

START

FINISH

Rhythm Value Maze 2
Page 17

START

FINISH

Tempo Maze
Page 20

▼ START

▼ FINISH

More Resources from D. Brian Weese!

Perplexing Puzzles

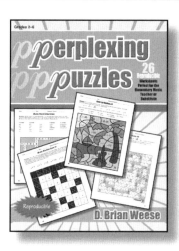

Grades 2–6 • Sssh, can you hear their musical minds turning? "Perplexing Puzzles" will keep your students quietly engaged while reinforcing musical concepts and terms. This book of twenty-six REPRODUCIBLE puzzles is leveled and includes worksheets for students in the second through sixth grades. With easy-to-follow directions, you can use these puzzles as part of your own instruction or leave them for a substitute with little musical background.

30/2587H   Reproducible Worksheets

Music Fundamentals

Grades 2–6 • You and your students will enjoy working your way through these forty-four fabulous, fundamentally sound, leveled, REPRODUCIBLE worksheets that reinforce melodic and rhythmic concepts. This jam-packed resource includes at least three different-leveled versions for every game, making it perfect for the music teacher or music substitute.

30/2557H   Reproducible Worksheets

More Music Fundamentals

Grades 2-6 • This collection of reproducible worksheets will challenge your students while providing you with valuable assessment pieces. Music concepts include writing rhythms based on syllables; matching melodic contours; identifying basic rhythmic notation, pitch notation, and music symbols; working with repeat signs, first and second endings, and da capo and dal segno symbols; and identifying time signatures.

30/2907H   Reproducible Worksheets